WANDERLUST

Los Angeles

A Creative Guide to the City

BETSY BEIER

WEST
MARGIN
PRESS

LOS ANGELES

46 SAN FERNANDO VALLEY

WESTSIDE

28

22

16

52

34

34

SANTA MONICA, PACIFIC PALISADES & MALIBU

40

MID CITY & MIRACLE MILE

PACIFIC OCEAN

N W E S

VENICE & SOUTH BAY BEACHES

40

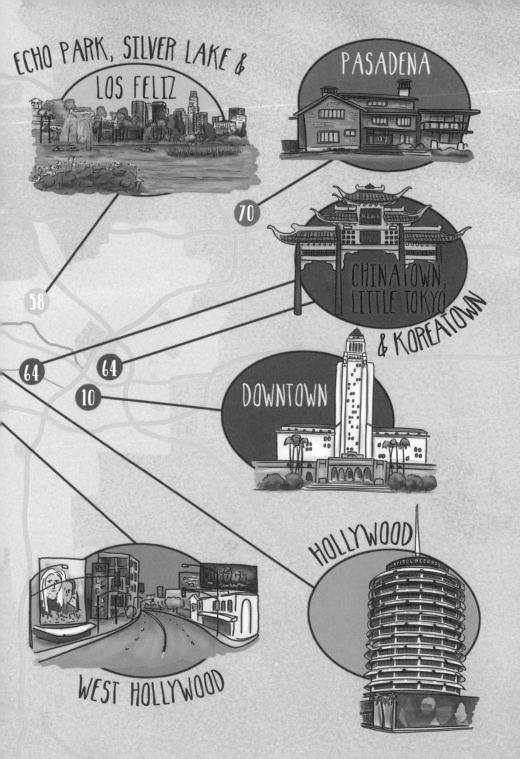

INTRODUCTION

INT. COFFEE SHOP AT HOLLYWOOD & VINE - MID MORNING
A film executive has only taken one sip of their coffee yet is eyeing the door, ready to leave. You have one last chance to sell your screenplay about a group of travelers coming to Los Angeles. They have their sights set on visiting all the well-known locations, yet crave something more from the elusive City of Angels.

FILM EXECUTIVE: (boredly) And why on earth do we need another movie about Los Angeles?

CLOSE-UP: Your mind swirls with colors and sounds of all your La La Land experiences. You've saved the best for last, and now is the time to give it your all.

YOU: (earnestly, yet dreamily) Just another movie about LA? No, this is not. I will show people why LA is named after the heavenly beings in the sky and why its number-one asset is emblazoned in 50-foot letters on a hillside. I will fascinate folks with the ooze in La Brea and the traffic jams that come out of nowhere at night. I will tell stories of star-watching by day along the Malibu shores, and stargazing at night in Griffith Park. I will take you to places around the world without a passport and be back home in time to watch the sun sink slowly into the Pacific Ocean. Why do we need another story about this town? Because it's Los Angeles. No other place like it in the world.

Stunned and intrigued, the film executive puts down their coffee.

FILM EXECUTIVE (slowly nodding their head): Hmmm, perhaps your story does need to be told. Let's make this happen...

GETTING STARTED

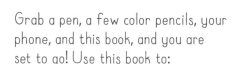

Grab a pen, a few color pencils, your phone, and this book, and you are set to go! Use this book to:

EXPLORE THE SIGHTS This book can be used as a travel guide before you head off on your journey or while you are actually at a location and looking around. Most chapters are about a specific neighborhood and some are citywide. Within each chapter, there is some high-level history, plus interesting facts and stories to give you a taste of the area. Just use the map on page 2 to look up the destination you are interested in exploring and head out the door!

JOURNAL & SKETCH YOUR EXPERIENCE I cherish the travel journals I have kept on my trips. Some are filled with watercolor scenes of our explorations, and others are just scribbled diaries of what we did that day. For me, a travel journal is not supposed to be perfect. It's an organic document of memories and stories while in a location. There's space throughout this book to write just the facts, and room to embellish your feelings and memories of the day.

PHOTO OP
Don't miss these photo opportunities! Look for this symbol throughout the book to find nearby sights for that perfect snapshot.

GET CREATIVE This book is all about getting creative and engaging in the local area you are exploring to have a unique and memorable experience. So if you have an inspiring idea, go for it! Some chapters provide artsy projects, some interactive games, while others encourage you to have fun with creative writing. The activities are meant to be spontaneous and entertaining. But you could also save the book activities until later in the day, perhaps at a cafe, or back at the hotel as you relive your adventures.

Enter: You!
To immerse yourself in the city best known for its film and entertainment industry, the activities in this book will help you step into the different roles on a film or TV production as you explore LA. Ready for some creative acting, writing, and drawing prompts? Lights, camera, *action!*

Now, it's time to get exploring!

ART SUPPLIES
I've learned over time that for packing art supplies, fewer is always better. A few black pens, a travel watercolor set, and a couple colored pencils are typically all I need. Occasionally, I'll bring along a glue stick or tape to add a unique wrapper, ticket stub, or scrap of paper I may find to my journal. You'll find plenty of room in the diary section for all these artistic and creative endeavors and any others you may think up!

THE GUIDE

PHOTO THEMES

A photo theme is a great way to see things you may not initially notice when touring a new spot. It's like a scavenger hunt to help you look beyond the sights and uncover the patterns and unique personality of a city. All you need is your phone and a theme—a color, an object, a style, an animal, etc. As you tour the city, hunt for your theme and snap a photo when you see it. By the end of the day, you may have taken ten pictures or hundreds of them.

Once you've taken all these fabulous pictures, you can make DIY souvenir gifts for yourself! Create an art collage using a multi-photo frame, or put it all together in an artsy photo book. Here are some possible photo themes you can use.

CAPTURE STAR-WORTHY MOMENTS

Embrace life in star-studded Los Angeles by taking celebrity-worthy photographs of you and your travel partners around town. Here are just a few ideal backdrops to be on the lookout for:

- Sunning yourself poolside on a clear blue afternoon
- Toasting at cocktail time at a trendy spot
- Posing against fabulous murals around town
- Toting shopping bags on Rodeo Drive
- Dancing at Griffith Observatory
- Holding your very own Oscar (from a souvenir shop!)
- Donning fabulous sunglasses on a palm-lined street
- Lounging on the beach at sunset

EMBRACE LOS ANGELES'S CAR CULTURE

Unlike many urban cities who embrace mass transportation, LA is obsessed with car culture. The only way to truly get around this massive region is by the freeways that crisscross the city, so while touring, pull out your phone and snap a few pictures that show some love for the automobile and driving!

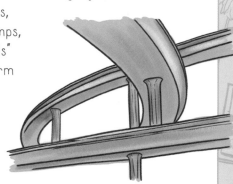

For instance, take photos and videos of freeway signs, traffic jams, high-end cars, convertibles, unique license plates, off-ramps, on-ramps, and even the infamous "spaghetti bowls" where major freeways connect and form massive curving arches of connecting lanes. At the end of your trip, edit the videos or collage your images together to create a story about the ubiquitous freeways and car enthusiasts of Los Angeles.

END FREEWAY ½ MILE

101 Hollywood

GIVE DRIVING DIRECTIONS LIKE A LOCAL

Although most freeways in Los Angeles have names (for example, I-405 is the San Diego Freeway, and the 110 is the Harbor Freeway), you will rarely hear Angelenos refer to them this way. Instead, everyone refers to freeways by starting with "the" and then the freeway number. So, Interstate 405 is "the 405," and US Route 101 is "the 101."

DOWNTOWN

Buzzing with noise and bustling with life, Downtown Los Angeles (DTLA) is the heart of the second-largest city in the US, after New York City. It is not only the historic center of the city, but also is brimming with entertainment and commerce. From the raucous, sometimes unruly pueblo days in the 1800s to the city sprawl (and exodus from the core) in the mid to late 1900s, DTLA has had its share of changes, yet with revitalization efforts over the last few decades there truly is a renaissance happening.

Los Angeles City Hall is at 200 N Spring Street.

TONGVA PEOPLES AND THE SPANISH

Long before the Spanish and Mexican arrived in the Los Angeles region, the Tongva Native American peoples (also known as Gabrieleño and Fernandeño people) inhabited the area. The largest of the Tongva villages was Yangna, whose center was where City Hall is now. Unbeknownst to the Tongva peoples, when the Spanish Empire conquered Mexico in 1521, the Spanish claimed the Los Angeles region (part of Alta California) as their territory of the Viceroyalty of New Spain.

In 1769, appointed Spanish governor Gaspar de Portolà explored the area and established a settlement known today as El Pueblo de Los Ángeles. The settlement grew to have 44 people by 1781 and survived primarily because of the labor of the local Tongva people. Meanwhile, Father Junipero Serra led his charge to create Catholic missions along the coast. In 1771 the first mission in the Los Angeles area, Mission San Gabriel Arcángel, was established, and two decades later Mission San Fernando was built. Life for the Tongva peoples would

Our Lady Queen of Angels Catholic Church is at 535 N Main Street.

never be the same. Within 50 years, almost all Native peoples of the region migrated to a missionary life of hard labor, plagued with diseases introduced by the Spanish.

When Mexico achieved independence from Spain in 1821, life began to change in the Los Angeles region as laws were passed to secularize missions. Many were converted to ranchos whose primary purpose was livestock and food production. Over the next three decades, the Mexican government gave over 400 land grants for ranchos from the sites of old missions as well as other areas. Names of some of the most prominent ranchos are still seen in cities, counties, and landmarks throughout Southern California, such as San Pedro, Simi, Los Feliz, La Brea, Topanga Malibu Sequit, and Los Palos Verdes.

THE GROWTH OF DOWNTOWN

Los Angeles experienced another dramatic change when Mexico ceded California to the United States at the end of the Mexican-American War in 1848 and gold was also discovered in Northern California. Settlers rushed to Southern California ranchos as the need for beef to feed the new inhabitants exploded. Businesses, hotels, a library, colleges, schools, and residences were built, and the area filled with horse-drawn streetcars and trolleys, then electric streetcars. Later the railroad connected downtown to San Pedro Bay, then to San Francisco, and finally across the county. By 1890, the small

EL PUEBLO DE LOS ÁNGELES & OLVERA STREET

Between North Alameda Street and Spring Street, El Pueblo de los Ángeles is known as the birthplace of Los Angeles. The area contains a central plaza dotted with statues and plaques discussing the city's history. A few of the buildings surrounding the plaza are some of the oldest in California, including Avila Adobe, La Iglesia de Nuestra Señora La Reina de Los Ángeles, and the Pico House, once a fancy hotel. Cutting through the Plaza on either side is Olvera Street, once called Wine Street, a pedestrian marketplace filled with vendors selling handicrafts, restaurants, and strolling musicians.

city had expanded to a metropolis of 50,000 people.

Despite the growing sprawl in the first half of the 1900s, DTLA remained the core of the city. Spring Street, dubbed the "Wall Street

Union Station is at 800 N Alameda Street.

of the West," was home to banking and financial institutions. Broadway welcomed theatres, vaudevilles, cinemas, and shopping. Grand Central Market opened in 1917 and offered fresh foods, meats, fish, baked goods, and more to the community, and is still in operation today. Hill Street, once named Calle de Toros or "Street of the Bulls" as bullfighting occurred there during Spanish occupation, was clogged with rail lines, bus lines, then automobiles through the commercial section. Atop the hill, beautiful Victorian residences looked down on the burgeoning city, with staircases and a funicular (Angels Flight, which operates today in a slightly different location) built to transport residents from their home to work.

Angels Flight stations are at 350 S Grand Ave. and 351 S Hill St.

In the latter half of the twentieth century, freeway networks exploded and people began to make their way out of downtown. Also, after almost 90 years of service, the interurban railway system of Yellow Cars and Red Cars (streetcars and trolley lines) stopped in 1963, which meant less people were traveling in and around the area.

Yet DTLA still bustled with business in the day. The Garment District (now known as the Fashion District) stayed busy manufacturing clothes, accessories, and textiles and selling wholesale and limited retail on Santee Alley. Many businesses on Hill Street transformed in the 1970s to form the Jewelry District. The Financial District moved from Spring Street to south of Bunker Hill where high-rises were being built. Manufacturing moved out to the suburbs or overseas, and empty

buildings became live/work spaces for artists, creating a newly formed Arts District. Even flower sales at the Los Angeles Flower Mart (and surrounding area known as the Flower District) blossomed all day with activity.

RENEWAL OF THE CITY

The twenty-first century brought revitalization to the area. In the South Park District you'll find the Convention Center, the Staples Center, and LA Live for anything from sporting events to concerts. The Arts District offers galleries and museums like the Museum of Contemporary Art, The Broad, and the Grammy Museum (at LA Live). The Los Angeles Music Center houses four massive venues, including the Walt Disney Concert Hall, and is where the Los Angeles Philharmonic and Los Angeles Opera perform. Given the sheer density of things to do and see in DTLA, it's hard to imagine that the area was once just a small pueblo of 44 people!

ARCHITECTURAL WONDERS OF DTLA

Many stunning buildings from the early 1900s still remain and are worth a visit to relive the feel of a bygone era.

BRADBURY BUILDING: Opened in 1893, LA's oldest commercial building has appeared in films like the 1982 *Blade Runner*.

CENTRAL LIBRARY: The Mediterranean Revival–style library built in 1926 expanded into a complex of buildings to become the third-largest library (in books and periodicals) in the country.

CITY HALL: The Neoclassical/Art Deco building, used in many films including the headquarters of the Daily Planet from the *Adventures of Superman* in the 1950s, was built in 1928 and remained the tallest building in Los Angeles until 1964.

UNION STATION: Built in 1939 in Art Deco/Mission Revival style, it became known as the "Last of the Great Railway Stations" and consolidated all the railroads into one terminal.

BRADBURY
BLDG

ENTER: Sound Designer

A sound designer acquires some or all sounds in a film and works with the film director to put together a soundtrack. The sound designer may also have to consider how to create sound effects like creaking stairs, a lightsaber, or a flying spaceship, many of which are created from everyday objects. For instance, the sound of a horse clomping down a road was created in the past by clapping coconut halves on gravel. And the sounds of a TIE fighter from *Star Wars* were made by combining elephant noises with a car driving on wet pavement!

Capture small soundbites with your phone—traffic noise, people walking, marketplaces, train station announcements, etc. Think of the story your audio might tell and write a movie synopsis to accompany your soundtrack.

CITY SOUNDBITES

Sound Recording _____   Location _____

Notes _____
_____

Sound Recording _____   Location _____

Notes _____
_____

Sound Recording _____   Location _____

Notes _____
_____

Sound Recording _____   Location _____

Notes _____
_____

THE STORY *behind your* SOUNDTRACK

DTLA PLAYLIST

Create a playlist (or score) for your movie. Did you hear any songs or musical tunes while you wandered the neighborhood from a passing car, or playing overhead while in a store or marketplace? Do sights around the area bring songs you know to mind? Compile your DTLA playlist below.

SONG

_____
_____
_____
_____
_____
_____
_____
_____
_____
_____
_____
_____
_____
_____
_____
_____

ARTIST

_____
_____
_____
_____
_____
_____
_____
_____
_____
_____
_____
_____
_____
_____
_____
_____

HOLLYWOOD

Driving through Hollywood you'll find streets named after ranchers and farmers (Ambrose Street, Gower Street, Hudson Avenue, Vine Street—after Cornelius Cole's vineyard) with a mix of eager real estate moguls (Wilcox Avenue, Beachwood Drive, Bronson Avenue, Taft Avenue). These settlers would probably never have guessed the land they were dividing up would become the epicenter for a whole new industry and home to some of the most famous people in the world in just a few short decades.

HOLLYWOOD BEFORE HOLLYWOOD

The Hollywood area was once called Cahuenga Valley, from the word Cabueng-ha, the name of the village where the local Gabrieleño tribe lived. It was located at the base of the Santa Monica foothills with prime access to a dirt road used for centuries by Native Americans to cut through the hills to the San Fernando Valley.

But with more settlers' arrivals, the adobes of the rancho days soon converted to farmhouses. Orchards, vineyards, and crops filled the large plots of land scattered in the area. In 1883, a devoutly religious Prohibitionist man named Harvey Wilcox moved from Kansas and decided to try ranching. He bought 150 acres of land and called his ranch Hollywood. Once he realized ranching wasn't his forté, he subdivided his land and submitted a grid map to the LA County recorder's office. This was the first document with the word "Hollywood" on it. With the new layout, homes began to be built, and the main street, Prospect Avenue (now Hollywood Boulevard), began to grow.

Around the same time, real estate developer H. J. Whitley (known as the "Father of Hollywood") bought large acres of land and developed an upscale residential community in the same area. He built the Hollywood Hotel (opened in 1902) and surrounded it with gardens of fragrant lemon groves and California pepper trees, attracting wealthy and society-driven guests. Hollywood now had a post office, a few markets, a hotel, and even a streetcar on Prospect Avenue. Soon after, the City of Hollywood was officially incorporated, then in 1910 it merged with Los Angeles.

The Hollywood Hotel is at 1160 N Vermont Avenue.

THE BIRTH OF A NEW INDUSTRY

In the 1890s, the first motion-picture cameras, the Kinetograph and the Cinématographe, were invented, giving way to a new art form. By the turn of the twentieth century, most films were made in New York, New Jersey, and Chicago. But seasonal weather drove directors to seek different locales to shoot films, and Los Angeles provided the perfect location: year-round sunshine, plenty of open land, and a side bonus of cheaper labor. In 1908, Selig Polyscope Company of Chicago completed the first film in Hollywood, *The Count of Monte Cristo*. By 1911, the first film studio, Nestor Film Company, opened on Sunset Boulevard and Gower Street. Within the year, more than 10 other studios opened.

There were early efforts to avoid crediting actors for their work. The first movie star to have her name outed was Florence Lawrence. After appearing in over 100 films and clips, audiences clambered to know her name. In an ingenious publicity stunt, a movie executive named Carl Laemmle took out a newspaper article stating the actor had died, only to retort with another article claiming Lawrence was alive and well. He blamed a rival studio company for the initial news, and his plan for publicity worked. The first movie star was officially born as everyone now knew her name! She and countless other actors paved the way for putting Hollywood on the map.

HOLLYWOODLAND & THE HOLLYWOOD HILLS

In 1923, streetcar moguls Eli Clark and "General" M.H. Sherman partnered with *Los Angeles Times* publisher Harry Chandler, Sidney Woodruff, and others to form a development group and touted the rugged canyon land above the flats of the newly forming Hollywood as the perfect spot to build storybook homes "above the turmoil of the city."* They named their new community Hollywoodland.

Chandler boldly put up a 50-foot-high sign on the hillside that blinked HOLLYWOODLAND to promote the development. At the time, the notion of a hillside community was a new concept. Without the equipment we have today, water, electricity, and sewage posed challenges in the hills. Yet the development was an instant success, and it is still highly coveted real estate today.

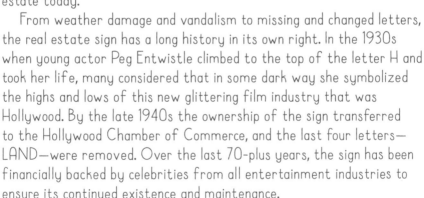

From weather damage and vandalism to missing and changed letters, the real estate sign has a long history in its own right. In the 1930s when young actor Peg Entwistle climbed to the top of the letter H and took her life, many considered that in some dark way she symbolized the highs and lows of this new glittering film industry that was Hollywood. By the late 1940s the ownership of the sign transferred to the Hollywood Chamber of Commerce, and the last four letters— LAND—were removed. Over the last 70-plus years, the sign has been financially backed by celebrities from all entertainment industries to ensure its continued existence and maintenance.

*This phrase comes from an advertisement in Chandler's *Los Angeles Times*, January 1924.

THE GOLDEN AGE OF HOLLYWOOD

When the silent-movie era ended, the Golden Age of Hollywood began. A new type of system was born where the movie studios were king and actors were required under contract to commit to just one. The Big 5, or the "majors," emerged: Metro Goldwyn Mayer, Warner Brothers Pictures, Paramount Pictures, 20th Century Fox, and RKO Pictures. Each studio essentially owned every aspect of their film making, from creative production to distribution. More importantly, they curated and groomed their list of leading actors. Many actors changed their names and were trained on everything, from speaking and dialect to singing, dancing, posture, or any number of physical activities required for a film. The stars had to look a certain way (through makeup, hair, fitness, even cosmetic surgery) and some were even told who to be romantically "involved" with.

GRAUMAN'S CHINESE THEATRE

Sid Grauman opened the Egyptian Theatre in 1922 to host the first Hollywood premiere, featuring Douglas Fairbanks in *Robin Hood*. Five years later, Grauman's Chinese Theatre opened and eventually grew more in fame when stars began to leave their mark in the cement outside.

Grauman's Chinese Theatre is at 6925 Hollywood Blvd.

HOLLYWOOD'S EXPANSION

The Golden Age of Hollywood ultimately ended when the Paramount Case of 1948 began to dismantle the exclusivity rights of studios. Hollywood was also expanding in the entertainment world with the rise of television in the 1950s as well as growth from the music recording industry. While studios spread out beyond Hollywood (except Paramount Studios), this didn't mean the end of Hollywood—just that it was beginning to grow, change, and evolve.

CAPITOL RECORDS BUILDING

Opened in 1956, this was the world's first circular office building, resembling a stack of records. If you watch, the red light at the top of the building continuously blinks "Hollywood" in Morse code! The Capitol Records Building is at 1750 Vine Street.

ENTER: Actor

An actor's main job is to translate a written character from a screenplay into an intriguing, captivating, convincing person on the screen or stage. To do so, they must first spend time understanding the characters, from their physical attributes to their hobbies, tastes, and quirks, and then interpret how best to portray those features by using physical movement, emotion, voice inflection, gestures, appearance, and other techniques.

Now's your chance to break into acting and be discovered! Try the acting exercises here and show off your skills. Have your friends or family traveling with you to join in on the fun!

Time Traveler

You, Harvey Wilcox, have just been transported through a time-travel machine from 1883 Hollywood and dropped onto Hollywood Boulevard today.

What is your initial reaction?

What would you say?

Who would you talk to?

Perform an improvisational monologue for a few minutes trying to figure out where you are. Engage people around you if you dare.

Be a Star

Live out your fantasy of living as a famous star by being one for five minutes. Fill out the character description cheat sheet below to create your celebrity persona. Get in character and talk, walk, and embody that star as you walk down the street. Have people in your group act as if you are a star as well.

Name:

Age:

Physical characteristics:

Originally from (i.e., accent in your voice):

Number of movies you've starred in:

Movie genre you're most famous for:

Your best fans:

WEST HOLLYWOOD

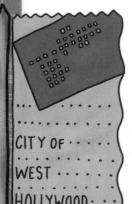

CITY OF WEST HOLLYWOOD

It's hard to believe West Hollywood (WeHo) is such a young city given its long history, distinct personality, and independent spirit. Surrounded by the affluent enclave of Beverly Hills and the mighty City of Los Angeles, WeHo's persistence in staying independent and unincorporated for so long was perhaps its most defining move in developing its unique, inclusive, spirited image today. So how did WeHo get its style?

A CITY CALLED SHERMAN

In 1890, streetcar mogul Moses Sherman bought a portion of land from one of the early ranchos, Rancho La Brea. His land development was the perfect location to join two of his interurban railway lines, ultimately connecting the City of Los Angeles to the small town along the beach, Santa Monica. He appropriately named his town Sherman and began utilizing the area for railroad shops, yards, and storage sheds. Many railroad employees also settled in the area to be close to their work. These railway days put the growing village on the map, and subsequently curious eyes took notice.

Many in the film industry in the early 1900s became attracted to Sherman as it was right next to Hollywood. Mary Pickford and her husband Douglas Fairbanks took advantage of the lesser-known area and established Pickford-Fairbanks Studio in 1922 on the corner of Santa Monica Boulevard and Formosa Avenue. (Their studio later became United Artists in 1927 and still exists today as The Lot.)

By 1925, the town name of Sherman didn't seem to fit anymore, and piggybacking off the success and notoriety of its neighbor, it was changed to West Hollywood. Although the City of Los Angeles grabbed up surrounding land as fast as it could, West Hollywood remained an unincorporated area of Los Angeles County, a factor that would ultimately help define its personality even today.

WEHO'S NEWFOUND POPULARITY

West Hollywood inadvertently became the top destination for the glitzy, glamorous nightlife scene of the most famous Hollywood stars. During Prohibition in the 1920s and early '30s, WeHo earned a reputation as a town with looser regulations (more liquor friendly) since it was immune to some of the laws, regulations, and stringent policing that was happening in the City of Los Angeles. This made the area quite attractive to many individualistic people of the time.

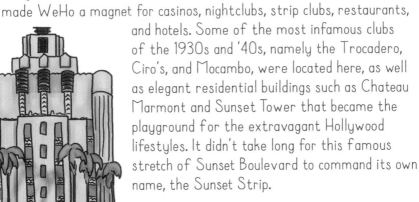

Chateau Marmont is at 8221 Sunset Boulevard.

Another reason for its explosion in popularity was its prime location. Sunset Boulevard, which runs from DTLA to the beach, just happens to be the main thoroughfare through West Hollywood. These factors combined made WeHo a magnet for casinos, nightclubs, strip clubs, restaurants, and hotels. Some of the most infamous clubs of the 1930s and '40s, namely the Trocadero, Ciro's, and Mocambo, were located here, as well as elegant residential buildings such as Chateau Marmont and Sunset Tower that became the playground for the extravagant Hollywood lifestyles. It didn't take long for this famous stretch of Sunset Boulevard to command its own name, the Sunset Strip.

The Sunset Tower Hotel is at 8358 Sunset Boulevard.

FROM CRIME TO COMMUNITY, MUSIC & ENTERTAINMENT

The Sunset Strip not only attracted glamorous stars looking to bend the rules, but also brought straight-up crooks like mobsters Mickey Cohen and Benjamin "Bugsy" Siegel. When Siegel left to Las Vegas, he allowed Cohen to grow his illegal operation by opening some unsuspicious shops like a haberdashery, a jewelry shop, and a custom shirt business as fronts for his booking and narcotics businesses. Cohen also blackmailed celebrities with their unwanted news or scandals. He finally found himself in San Francisco's notorious Alcatraz prison for tax evasion.

The liberal environment and bustling nightlife on the Sunset Strip and in West Hollywood during the 1940s became an attractive haven for another minority group, gays and lesbians. Because being gay was treated a crime, the lax attitude of policing in WeHo was a huge relief to the LGBTQ community as police raids of gay establishments and persecution were common occurrences of the time. Although some of the clubs on the Strip were not outwardly called gay nightclubs, there were plenty of gay patrons and others who celebrated the scene.

Then in the 1960s and '70s, a new raucous scene on the Strip developed, this time from the music industry. With droves of hippies and new clubs opening, the counterculture movement of the time coincided with many emerging bands like The Doors, The Byrds, The Kinks, and Led Zeppelin who made their names at nightclubs such as The Troubadour, Whisky a Go Go, and The Roxy. The music scene in the area continued into the '80s with punk rock, new wave, and heavy metal bands like Van Halen and Mötley Crüe performing to wild, untamed partiers, a trait that became a signature aspect of the Sunset Strip.

THE SUNSET STRIP

West Hollywood

With pressure from what would seem like an incongruous crowd of WeHo residents—Russian Jews, senior citizens, and the LGBTQ+ community—and coinciding with rent-control measures—West Hollywood finally became an incorporated city in 1984. Immediately following, the citizens elected the first city council in the country with an openly gay majority. West Hollywood became known as not only one of the most prominent LGBTQ+ cities in the US but also one of the most progressive cities regarding public policy. The WeHo community is active in social movements of all kinds, from rights for all (human, civil, women's, LGBTQ+, animals) to environmental issues. It's easy to see why this fun-loving (and perhaps slightly indulgent) city has such a positive image.

MELROSE AVENUE

Melrose Avenue became the happening place to shop in the 1980s, sporting the coolest fashions, eyewear, records, accessories, and used clothing, touting all the latest trends from new wave to rockabilly. The apex to the area's popularity culminated with the seven-years-long television series in the '90s *Melrose Place*, set in West Hollywood and more specifically in and around Melrose Avenue. The trends from those decades have changed, but the area hasn't lost its cool.

ENTER: Movie Promoter

A movie promoter must create a strong promotional campaign through advertising, marketing, public relations, franchising, and merchandising for a film to be successful. The stakes can also be quite high, as the marketing budget for films can sometimes equal almost half the cost of production! Yet if done correctly and early before the film's release, the reward can pay off in ticket sales, attention, and awards.

You've been tasked to design billboards that will display along Sunset Boulevard for the following blockbuster releases. Your goal is to persuade people to see the films using large lettering for the title, key illustrations featuring the main character and/or location, names of the featured actors, and a tagline for the movie. Using the creative briefs here, design billboards that will stop traffic and drive people to the theaters.

BILLBOARD #1
TITLE: The Chateau
GENRE: Horror
TAGLINE: *"Nobody will be checking out when Lulu arrives."*
DESCRIPTION: When one guest's pet Chihuahua begins to exponentially grow, other hotel guests of the Chateau Marmont in West Hollywood start to disappear. Can the staff stop Cory's dog before it's too late?

BILLBOARD #2

TITLE: Sunrise on Sunset
GENRE: 1970s Romance
TAGLINE: *"Her words. His tunes.
Together, they can change the world."*
DESCRIPTION: An introverted writer and a hippie guitarist find
love at the Viper Room, but when the sun comes up things change.
Can love and peace outweigh the lure of fame and fortune?

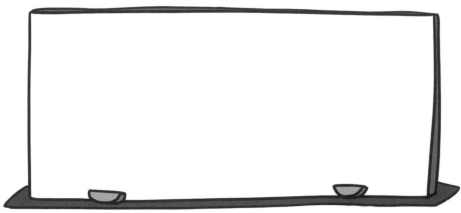

BILLBOARD #3 - DESIGN YOUR OWN

TITLE:
GENRE:
TAGLINE:
DESCRIPTION:

WESTSIDE

The Westside communities of Beverly Hills, Bel Air, Holmby Hills, and Brentwood are home to some of the wealthiest people in the world. The massive mansions, the elegant hotels, and the high-end boutiques that line Rodeo Drive make the ultimate place for people-watching and gleaning the latest in fashion, hair, makeup, and more! Spending a relaxing afternoon on the Westside may give us that tiny taste of the glamorous life we all secretly crave.

AGRICULTURAL BEGINNINGS

The Westside of LA has always been a sought-after location to live, long before the enormous homes and fancy shops arrived. The area had one thing that many other parts of Los Angeles did not: water. In fact, the Tongva peoples lived here for centuries and named the area the Gathering of the Waters. In the mid to late 1800s, the land was used in farming, cattle, sheep, and oil, changing hands many times because of, ironically, droughts. By the end of the 1800s there was even a pair of developers who hoped to establish a North African—themed subdivision called Morocco for this area.

WEALTH, GLITZ & GLAM

At the turn of the twentieth century, oilman and developer Burton Green purchased "Morocco" and named the area Beverly Hills, after his wife's suggestion to name it after Beverly Farms in Massachusetts. Landscape architect Wilbur Cook designed wide, curving streets and created an "emerald necklace" or garden of greenspace partially surrounding the streets (now Beverly Gardens Park). In 1912, the Beverly Hills Hotel opened and became the center of socializing for the new Hollywood film industry. Rodeo Drive was then actually a humble bridle path that took the stars to the hotel from Santa Monica and Wilshire Boulevards.

During the first half of the 1900s, Beverly Hills grew immensely. The "Golden Triangle" was formed by the intersection of Santa Monica and Wilshire Boulevard and buzzed with new businesses serving the local community including Rodeo Drive. Up in the hills enormous mansions and estates were developed, and down on the flats a new Italian Renaissance City Hall opened in 1931. But it wasn't until the latter half of the century that Beverly Hills and the Westside communities really began to sparkle and evolve into what we currently recognize.

The Beverly Hills Hotel, also known as the "Pink Palace," is at 9641 Sunset Boulevard.

MANSIONS OF THE PLATINUM TRIANGLE

Neighboring Beverly Hills, Bel Air, and Holmby Hills, nicknamed the Platinum Triangle, are home to some of the most expensive (and expansive) homes around the world. Even though most of these mansions cannot be seen from the road, there are plenty of photographs online and film cameos that will give you a taste of just how big these dwellings go!

GREYSTONE MANSION: This mansion built in 1928 was given as a gift to the son of oilman Edward Doheny. The son, Ned, died only five months after moving in due to an apparent murder-suicide by his personal friend. Later, Ned's wife sold the mansion to Paul Trousdale, who kept Greystone intact but divided the rest of the land to form the exclusive area called Trousdale Estates. Greystone is now owned by the City of Beverly Hills and can be toured.

PLAYBOY MANSION: Located in Holmby Hills, the Playboy Mansion has seen its fair share of celebrities and stars when former owner Hugh Hefner used to throw extravagant parties and gatherings. After Hefner's passing, the mansion was sold in 2016 to businessman and investor Daren Metropoulos. The mansion is protected by the City of Los Angeles from demolition.

TROUSDALE ESTATES: This area of Beverly Hills, once Doheny Ranch and Greystone Mansion, was purchased by Paul Trousdale in 1956 and developed into an exclusive neighborhood of well-appointed homes favored by many stars from the past—such as Ray Charles, Dean Martin, Frank Sinatra, and Elvis Presley—as well as the present—such as Jennifer Aniston, Cindy Crawford, and Vera Wang.

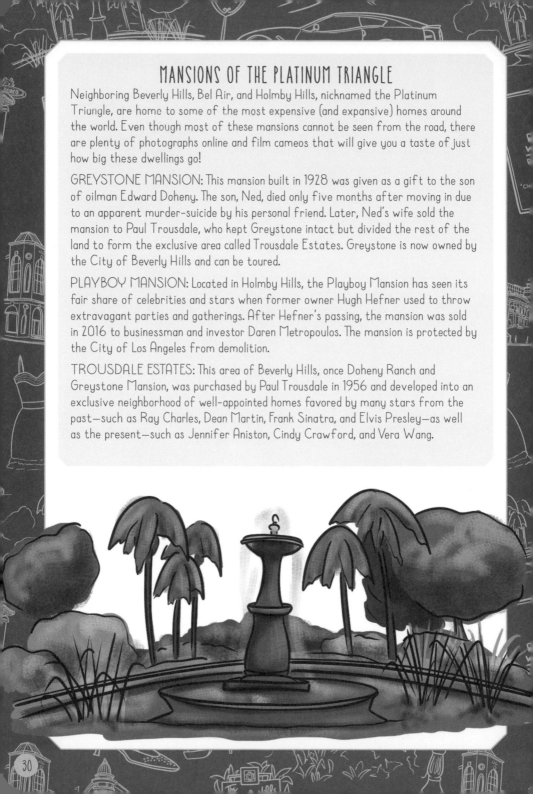

RODEO DRIVE

Rodeo Drive remained relatively ordinary up until the 1960s when Fred Hayman saw much more potential. In 1964 he opened the first luxury shop, Giorgio Beverly Hills, and soon many followed. By the late '70s, PR campaigns touted Rodeo Drive as "the shopping place for the rich and famous" as well as "the best shopping in the world." Over the next few decades more enhancements were made to the street, namely Two Rodeo Drive, an outdoor carless shopping street reminiscent of an old European street, yet brimming with high-end brands such as Versace, Tiffany & Co., and Jimmy Choo.

For some, Rodeo Drive represents the pinnacle of what life is like in Los Angeles. The palm tree–lined road, manicured flowers and plants, parked luxury cars, and high-end boutiques overwhelmingly exude an air of wealth and glamour seen in films and television as quintessentially Hollywood. With a stroll down Rodeo Drive, you never know what latest Hollywood star or longtime celebrity out and about on a shopping trip you might see.

WALK OF STYLE

Conceived by Fred Hayman, the Walk of Style along Rodeo Drive celebrates creatives in fashion, design, and costuming. Giorgio Armani was the first to be honored with many other fashion giants following, such as Gianni and Donatella Versace, Manolo Blahnik, and Valentino Garavani. The walk also recognizes Oscar-winning costume designers such as Catherine Martin, Edith Head, and Milena Canonero. The Walk of Style is on Rodeo Drive from Wilshire Boulevard to South Santa Monica Boulevard.

ENTER: Costume Designer

A costume designer in film or television production is in charge of designing, creating, and acquiring all costumes for actors and extras. Their job helps define the characters' personalities and provides context to the era in which the production depicts. Their work also needs to take into consideration the movement of the actors, and the clothes need to be durable enough to last through months of filming.

You are the costume designer for two new film concepts. Look for fashion inspiration along Rodeo Drive, and don't forget accessories!

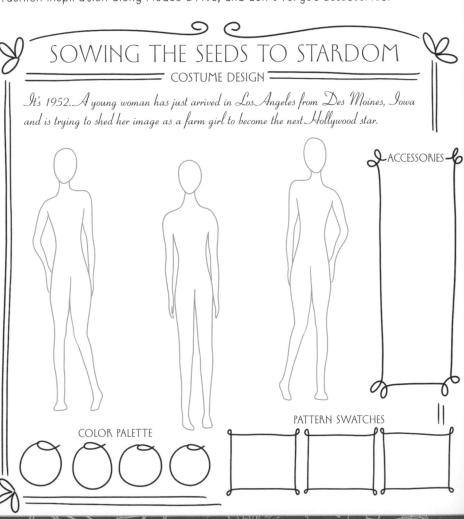

SOWING THE SEEDS TO STARDOM
COSTUME DESIGN

It's 1952. A young woman has just arrived in Los Angeles from Des Moines, Iowa and is trying to shed her image as a farm girl to become the next Hollywood star.

ACCESSORIES

COLOR PALETTE

PATTERN SWATCHES

INDIVIDUALIST EXTINCTION

COSTUME DESIGN

set in los angeles in the year 2099, this futuristic thriller depicts a clash between ultra-modern hollywood eccentrics and stylish, simplistic clones.

COLOR PALETTE

PATTERN SWATCHES

ACCESSORIES

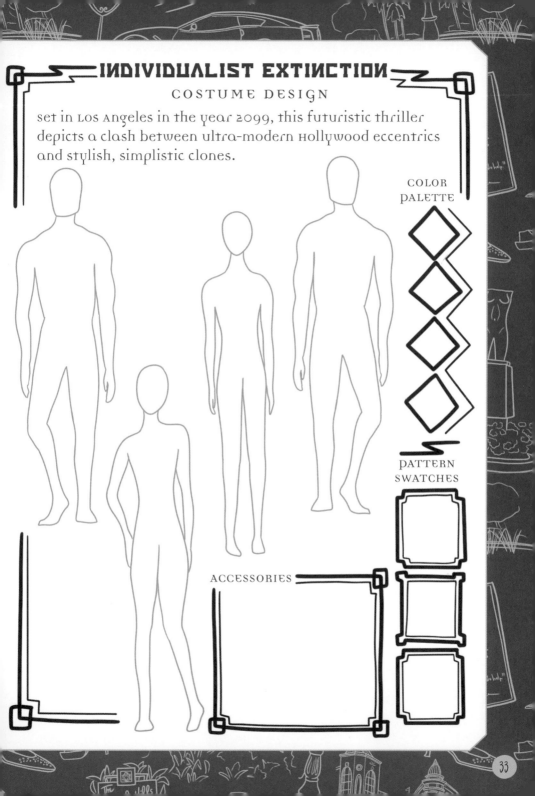

SANTA MONICA, PACIFIC PALISADES & MALIBU

It's hard to picture the initial intent for Santa Monica as an industrial port city. Mining and ranching entrepreneurs Colonel Robert S. Baker and Senator John P. Jones purchased this land and started auctioning

The Santa Monica Pier is down Colorado Avenue at its intersection with Ocean Avenue.

off the first town lots in 1875. They built a railroad line along the beach and a pier where steamers from San Francisco arrived. As time passed, it became apparent industry was not the best use of this area. The growing population of Los Angeles at the turn of the twentieth century sought out the coast for entertainment. Hotels, bathhouses, plunge pools, casinos, ballrooms, sports clubs, and pleasure piers soared in popularity as Angelenos flocked to the beaches. Capitalizing on these beach resort assets, the Santa Monica we know today was born.

SANTA MONICA PIER

At the end of Route 66 lies the oldest pleasure pier on the West Coast, Santa Monica Pier. Opened in 1909, the original cement municipal pier did not have any attractions or amenities, but visitors still came to stroll along the promenade in the ocean air. (Ironically, this pier's main function was to take sewage pipes out beyond the breakers!)

SANTA MONICA

66

End of the Trail

Santa Monica's municipal cement pier proved unable to hold up to the elements and was replaced by the current wooden pier around 1920. At the same time, an additional pier was added alongside the municipal pier. Charles I.D. Looff, the amusement ride developer and carousel builder who established Coney Island in New York, Asbury Park in New Jersey, and Crescent Park in Rhode Island, saw the opportunity to take his talents and develop pleasure piers along the West Coast. Looff and his son built the Moorish-style "hippodrome" building for his ornate carousel,

which still exists, as well as a wooden roller coaster and two other thrill rides.

These were a hit—until the Great Depression. By the 1930s, the pier was mainly used as a ferry landing and fishing as the attractions were sold off. Besides the famous entry gate (built in 1938), development on the pier remained stagnant for decades with plans for removal in the early 1970s. Hollywood saved the day when the famous Hippodrome and Looff's gorgeous carousel were seen in the popular movie *The Sting*. This new enthusiasm as well as residents' support to save the pier put demolition on hold. Santa Monica Pier was refurbished and reopened as a year-round family amusement park called Pacific Park in 1996.

Today the pier remains one of LA's top attractions. It features a roller coaster, rides for adults and children, games, restaurants, shops, and the iconic Ferris wheel that can be seen for miles, Pacific Wheel. It has been featured in hundreds of movies and television shows and radiates Southern California beach resort culture as we know it!

OTHER SANTA MONICA FAVORITES

East of the pier is the famous Third Street Promenade, where many world-famous performers including Andy Grammar first got their start. This three-block, pedestrian-only, open air shopping street hosts street performers, restaurants, a weekly farmers market, and more. And right by the beach and open to the public sits the Annenberg Community Beach House. Once an elaborate estate of actor Marion Davies and media tycoon William Randolph Hearst, the facility has a splash pool, playground, beach courts, and even a restored guest house.

There is also Tongva Park, named after the Native peoples in the LA region. This six-acre park features native landscaping to Southern California, walking paths, a children's play structure, and gorgeous viewing platforms overlooking the Pacific Ocean. With all the entertainment, food, and nature, it's no wonder Santa Monica draws visitors from around the world.

Third Street Promenade is between Wilshire Boulevard and Broadway.

PACIFIC PALISADES

Near Santa Monica and located in the Westside, Pacific Palisades is a mostly residential neighborhood home to gorgeous homes, clubs, parks, and beaches. Many parts of Pacific Palisades has been filmed in movies, television, and even music videos. For instance, Palisades High School was featured in *Modern Family, Freaky Friday, Crazy/Beautiful, Carrie, Teen Wolf,* and many others!

Also in the area is the beautiful Getty Villa. As one of two locations of the J. Paul Getty Museum, the Getty Villa celebrates Greek, Roman, and Etruscan culture, arts, architecture, and history, and even has beautiful gardens with plants that the ancient Romans cultivated.

The Getty Villa is at 17985 Pacific Coast Highway.

MALIBU

Once dubbed the Riviera of America, Malibu is home to world-famous movie stars and entertainers, and maintains a tantalizing lore for most outsiders. Nostalgic Malibu Pier has some shopping, equipment rentals, charter boats, and nearby food options, while adjacent Surfrider Beach offers some of the best surfing in the world.

The most popular beach in the area is El Matador Beach, tucked below an eroded bluff (stairs from atop give access to the beach) and decorated with eroded rocks and caves along the beach itself. It's a popular surf spot and attracts all kinds of photographers, from professional model shoots to tourists capturing the sunset.

Malibu also provides access to Topanga State Park, the world's largest wildland within a major city. With extensive hiking, biking, and horseback riding trails, this state park is a popular spot to get away from the hectic LA traffic and into nature.

SANTA MONICA PIER ON SCREEN

Have you spotted the Santa Monica Pier in any of these movies and television shows that featured it?

MOVIES
- A Night at the Roxbury
- Forrest Gump
- Her
- Titanic
- Pacific Rim: Uprising

TELEVISION
- Charlie's Angels
- Grey's Anatomy
- Criminal Minds
- Modern Family
- 24

ENTER: Cinematographer

A cinematographer (also known as DP, DoP, or Director of Photography) makes artistic and technical decisions regarding the image to ultimately capture the director's vision of how the film should look and convey the story written by the screenwriter. Artistically, a cinematographer determines camera placement and movement, as well as shot composition, lighting, size, and focus. Technically, they choose the proper camera, lens, and filters, as well as inform the lighting crew how to light the scene to capture the story.

You are the cinematographer for a new short film about the Santa Monica Pier. Your goal is to not only capture the essence of the Pier itself, but also document the story of life on the oldest pleasure pier on the West Coast. On the next page, plan your shots to show the world the joyful rides, the colorful games, the classic foods, and the crowds of people enjoying their time at the beach.

Alternately, imagine the pier is haunted and change your style to capture this spooky feel. Play with lighting, angles, framing, and filters to create the mood of the film. Then compile your imagery into a slideshow or movie and watch your documentary debut.

SHOT LIST
☆ A DAY at the PIER ☆

SHOT TYPE	DESCRIPTION	NOTES CAMERA MOVEMENT, ACTIONS, LOCATION, ETC.	DONE
WIDE SHOT OR LONG SHOT	provide context for where your subject is with the background and surroundings		
MEDIUM SHOT OR WAIST SHOT	capture your subject at medium distance		
LOW-ANGLE SHOT	give a sense of power by taking a shot looking up		
HIGH-ANGLE SHOT	give a sense of vulnerability by taking a shot looking down		
OVER-THE-SHOULDER SHOT	show a new perspective by capturing the view behind the shoulder of someone out of frame		
EYE-LEVEL SHOT	capture a scene directly looking in someone's eyes		
CLOSE-UP SHOT	get all the details by capturing your subject at close range		
POINT-OF-VIEW SHOT	show a personal perspective by capturing what your subject sees		

VENICE & SOUTH BAY BEACHES

Venice and the South Bay Beaches of Los Angeles are full of personality, character—and characters! These spots radiate LA's beach lifestyle and are the ideal spot to truly experience SoCal's hip culture in action.

VENICE OF AMERICA

In the late 1800s, well-traveled businessman and conservationist Abbot Kinney saw much potential in the Santa Monica area. He first built a tennis court, then partnered in a tract of land along the coast to create a resort and entertainment paradise called Ocean Park; but his greatest success was converting swampy lands slightly inland from the beach into what would be his creative Venice of America.

On July 4, 1905, Venice of America opened to the public. Kinney's goal was to create a resort area that not only entertained visitors but also sparked the Old World charm of Venice, Italy. The development capitalized on canals as a source of transportation, complete with gondolas and Italian-singing gondoliers. Along with the canals were: a miniature railroad; amusement piers with entertainment and shops; Venetian-inspired buildings, hotels, and cottages; yacht racing and swim competitions in a large lagoon; live musical concerts; and even fireworks. With the help of the trolley cars and railroads from DTLA, Venice of America drew upwards of 100,000 tourists on the weekends! Later, another set of canals called the Short Line Canals were dug to connect to the Grand Canal.

By the 1920s, automobile popularity grew and infrastructure in Venice was in disrepair. Many of the attractions of Venice of America closed and most of the canals were filled in to pave more roads. (The canals that still exist are from the Short Line extension.) At the same time, oil was also discovered in the area, leaving the remaining canals clogged and fetid with waste and debris. The once popular vision of Kinney's remained neglected until the 1990s, when the canals were renovated and reopened as a desirable residential part of the city.

Today you can stroll along the canals of Venice to see the cute houses mixed with new modern gems. Many owners have small boats or canoes tied up outside their home, proving that the canals still give people great pleasure!

ABBOT KINNEY BOULEVARD

Named after the creator of Venice of America, Abbot Kinney Boulevard is filled with restaurants, bars, shops, boutiques, and loads of picture-perfect spots that exude bohemian coolness.

SURFING LEGENDS AND LA SURF CULTURE

Surfing wasn't invented in LA, but surf culture did boom once it arrived in Southern California!

The story goes that at the turn of the twentieth century, railroad tycoon Henry Huntington devised a publicity stunt to promote ridership along his Pacific Electric Railway trolley. Huntington hired

Hawaiian surf legend George Freeth to time his wave riding according to the train schedule such that when the train passed by the coast, he'd be visible. The stunt worked, and curiosity was sparked.

A few years later Olympic silver medalist and fellow Hawaiian Duke Kahanamoku also fascinated crowds in Santa Monica with his surfing. Hollywood got wind of Kahanamoku and casted him in several movies. When he wasn't filming, he surfed at the beach. Soon, bare-chested male athletes (an uncommon sight in the first several decades of the 1900s) became the norm and a whole new culture of surfer boys began.

But what really sent surfing off to a different level was a woman named Gidget! Screenwriter Frederick Kohner wrote novels after hearing stories from his teenage daughter about life with her surfer friends on the beaches of Malibu. Inspired by the books, the *Gidget* movie was a hit. The beach lifestyle went well beyond just the sport of surfing and bled into everyday life through products, fashion, and music. To some, the commercialization of their free-spirit surf culture was tinged with irony, yet others embraced the popularity and used it to their advantage to promote other agendas like environmental issues.

SOUTH BAY BEACHES
Soak in the sun at any of these beaches in the area.

Dockweiler	Hermosa
El Porto	Redondo
Manhattan	Torrance

The Venice Public Art Walls are on Ocean Front Walk.

BODYBUILDERS ON MUSCLE BEACH

Muscle Beach originated back in the 1930s just down the way on the beach in Santa Monica. As part of the Works Progress Administration (WPA) programs of the era, exercise equipment was installed on the beach. The equipment immediately became popular with gymnasts and acrobats. Soon came the bodybuilders to the scene, such as Vic Tanny, Jack LaLanne, and Joe Gold.

Many of these bodybuilders were part of the Hollywood scene as stunt people and actors, which only increased the popularity of Muscle Beach as a place to watch these athletic people "perform." By the 1950s a second bodybuilding/fitness area along the beach opened in Venice, officially named "Muscle Beach Venice." It was smaller in size and was more focused on weightlifting than gymnastics and acrobatics.

SKATEBOARDING

Skateboarding, first called "sidewalk surfing," is said to have originated in California sometime in the 1950s when surfers were looking for something to do when there were no waves to be surfed. The first skateboards were pretty raw, most likely just a board with some type of roller skate wheels.

Venice Skatepark is at 1800 Ocean Front Walk.

ENTER: Casting Director

A casting director is a matchmaker of sorts. They meticulously read the script and work with the producers and directors to understand the type of actors they would like for each role in a film. They then organize and plan auditions for a select list of candidates, and hold casting calls to fill potentially hundreds of characters in a film, from lead roles to extras. On the other side they also negotiate salary and contract details with actors and their agents.

Your job is to cast all the roles in the next smash surfer movie, *Hermosa Dawn Patrol*. Use the casting call sheet to understand the characters needed in the film. Look around and make notes or sketches of potential people you may find to fill the roles below: their clothes, mannerisms, overheard conversations. Why might they be the perfect fit?

EXTRA CREDIT

Ask your family or friends or approach other people you think would play along to "try out" for one of the following roles. Have them perform an improvisational speech based on the notes below, then decide if you would hire them!

COOPER: *Cooper has just had the best ride of their life at a local surf competition, yet misses life in Chicago. Walking back up the beach with their board, they see Koa and compares life in the city to life among the waves.*

SLATER: *Hanging in the water beyond the break with their crowd at dawn patrol, Slater berates Cooper as a poser.*

DAIZE: *Remembering her days growing up in a commune, Ms. Layne tries to explain the beauty of LA's surf culture to Mr. Larsen.*

CASTING CALL
HERMOSA DAWN PATROL

Summary: A Chicago city-kid moves to LA and lucks out with natural surfing abilities, much to the dismay of the extremely competitive locals of the South Bay beaches. Can the older generation who defined the laid back surf culture help keep the waters calm as the younger generation competes for top prize?

NAME/ROLE	DESCRIPTION	NOTES
COOPER / LEAD ROLE	A kid from Chicago whose family moved to Hermosa Beach, much to their dismay. On a dare, Cooper surfs on a stormy day. To everyone's surprise, they kill it. They're now the surf champion of the state, yet in a world of outdoorsy surfer culture, Cooper can't seem to shake their urban roots.	
KOA / SUPPORTING ROLE	The one true friend of Cooper and another transplant to Los Angeles, having grown up on the small Hawaiian island of Lanai. Despite their opposite backgrounds and outlooks on life, Koa and Cooper are inseparable.	
SLATER / SUPPORTING ROLE	Cooper's archenemy. They spent their entire life training to be a surf pro, yet Cooper is better.	
MR. LARSEN / SUPPORTING ROLE	Cooper's stressed-out dad. He works in finance and is like a fish out of water when he's at the beach.	
MS. LAYNE / SUPPORTING ROLE	Slater's mom who grew up in a hippie commune. She loves everyone she meets yet is blinded by Slater's evil ways.	
SURFER DUDES & CHICKS / EXTRAS	Slater's surf pals.	
RANDOM LOCALS / EXTRAS	People to represent the location in a crowd scene or in the background.	

SAN FERNANDO VALLEY

In the mid-1800s, fruit crates with beautifully illustrated labels of orange groves of the San Fernando Valley and other areas in Southern California were sent across the entire country by railroad, essentially becoming an advertisement for the West. Fast forward over 150 years, the Valley is now home to many of the major studio companies' soundstages and backlots. The *Friends* living room of Monica and Rachel's apartment in the West Village of NYC is actually in Burbank. Both the overgrown, dinosaur-infested amusement park in *Jurassic Park* and the quaint city of Hill Valley in *Back to the Future* are in Universal City. It's amazing how real these places feel despite being shot not on location but in the backstage studio lands on a set!

VALLEY ACCESS AND WATER

In the 1800s, the spacious San Fernando Valley just over Cahuenga Pass through the Hollywood Hills was filled with ranchos and farms. Throughout history, water has always been an issue for the Valley, the inconsistencies in waterflow resulting in floods and droughts. The lack of access from railroads and stagecoach traffic limited growth as well.

Things began to change during the latter half of the 1800s when the railroad lines came and roads were carved to better connect the Valley with the outside world. Noting the persistent water problems, civil engineer and head of LA water system William Mulholland and his cohorts decided to take matters into their own hands. In some underhanded dealings, they piped water from 250 miles away to provide for the Valley and the rest of Los Angeles. This now fertile land became a boom for development. Housing tracts were planned, roads were laid out, and cattle farms were displaced.

Moviemakers like Universal Pictures founder Carl Laemmle also saw potential in making this area a permanent facility—and thus, Universal City was born.

UNIVERSAL STUDIOS

Universal City is home to Universal Studios' film studio and backlot, most of NBC Universal's West Coast television and news broadcasting (KNBC, NBC News, Telemundo), a "CityWalk" promenade of restaurants, shops and cinemas, and the first Universal Studios Theme Park.

The backlot of Universal contains many well-known streets and scenes seen in movies and television shows, including Colonial Street from *Desperate Housewives*, Courthouse Square from *Back to the Future*, New York Street and Modern New York Street, Bates Motel, and various roads and alleys where possibly murders or chase scenes in your favorite shows have occurred! The public can also visit the amusement park to experience films and shows in person.

WARNER BROS. STUDIOS

Located in Burbank in the Valley, Warner Bros. Studios was founded in 1923 by brothers Sam, Harry, Albert, and Jack Warner. It has over time added other entertainment such as television, animation (Warner Bros. Animation and Cartoon Network Studios), and video games. In the 1970s, Warner Bros. formed a venture with Columbia Pictures to create The Burbank Studios (TBS), also in Burbank. Old shows such as *The Dukes of Hazzard, Fantasy Island*, and *The Waltons* have credits at the end noting they were filmed at The Burbank Studios.

Warner Bros. also has numerous backlot

sets and soundstages on site. Some of the sets include a New York street, "Warner Village," a French street, a Midwest business and residential street, and a jungle lagoon. The Warner Bros. Studio Tour Hollywood (located in Burbank, despite the name) welcomes the public to tour soundstages for famous TV shows and backlots, as well as view props, costumes, and more.

WALT DISNEY STUDIOS

Walt Disney Studios, located on 51 acres of land in Burbank, moved to this location (from a variety of other locations in Los Angeles) following the release of *Snow White and the Seven Dwarfs* in 1927. Apparently the money made from that film made the move possible. The main use of the location at the time was for animation, from ink and paint departments to post-production buildings. Live-action filming evolved later in the decades at this location.

Walt Disney Studios also offers backlot and soundstage production facilities to production companies for rental. This facility is not open to the public, yet Disney fans shouldn't be dismayed since Disneyland in Anaheim is just down the way!

STUDIO RANCHES

Many of the major film studios own or share "ranches" or acres of land in other areas around Southern California for filming. For instance, Disney's Golden Oak Ranch is located in Placerita Canyon. Old films, such as *Old Yeller* and *The Parent Trap*, and newer films, such as *Pirates of the Caribbean II* and *Pearl Harbor*, have been filmed here. Ranch locations provide film companies more space to film that a small backlot cannot.

HOME OF THE BRADY BUNCH

Although the 1970s TV show *The Brady Bunch* was filmed entirely on set, they used an actual house in Studio City as the model for the family's home. Recently HGTV bought it and completely renovated the home to look like the actual set. The Brady Bunch House is at 11222 Dilling Street.

CBS STUDIO CENTER

Another large studio located in the Valley is CBS Studio Center. This location began in 1928 as Keystone Studios when it outgrew its Silver Lake location. Many films and television shows have been shot in these soundstages and backlot including oldies like *Gilligan's Island*, *The Mary Tyler Moore Show*, and more recent shows such as *Will & Grace*, *Brooklyn Nine-Nine*, and *Parks and Recreation*.

MORE AND MORE STUDIOS

There are two more studios around Los Angeles you could tour. Paramount Studios, founded in 1912, is the oldest and last remaining studio in Los Angeles proper. Its facilities are located on Melrose Avenue.

There's also Sony Pictures Studios, located in Culver City. It has filmed classics like *The Wizard of Oz* and *Singin' in the Rain* as well as more modern shows like *Breaking Bad* and *The Amazing Spider-Man*.

ENTER: Set Designer

A set designer designs and creates the environment or set for a film. They draw up plans of models of the sets based on the overall theme, genre, era, mood, and intent of the film. Their floor plans and models show not only the layout but also indicate details such as furniture, drapery, styling, and large props needed to tell the story.

You are the set designer for a new television show about a group of three friends who live together in Los Angeles. They are passionate about social justice issues and lead their community with their convictions, yet pine for simpler days when they lived at home with their parents and things were taken care of by others. How do you design the furniture and decoration to imbue the friends' spirit while also evoking nostalgia from their childhood years? Be sure to add notes and details that shouldn't be missed.

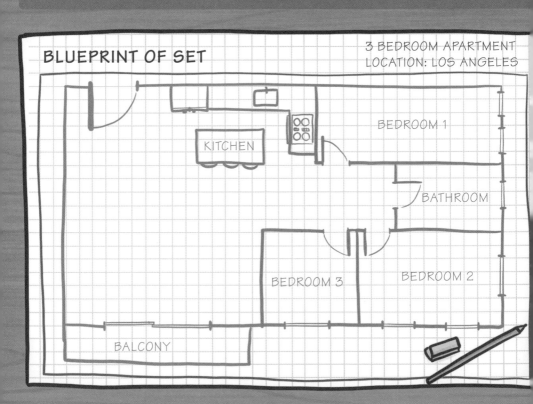

BLUEPRINT OF SET

3 BEDROOM APARTMENT
LOCATION: LOS ANGELES

KITCHEN

BEDROOM 1

BATHROOM

BEDROOM 3

BEDROOM 2

BALCONY

SKETCH OF LIVING ROOM

DETAIL SKETCHES &
NOTES OF ACCESSORIES/DECORATIVE ITEMS

MID CITY
& MIRACLE MILE

Miracle Mile, Mid City, and surrounding neighborhoods have been a connecting point, in some sense, that ties the whole LA region together. Though not as well known, these neighborhoods historically, architecturally, and culturally tell the story of the history of the area through the parks, buildings, museums, and people who live here.

PREHISTORIC LOS ANGELES & LA BREA TAR PITS

Long before people inhabited the Los Angeles area, mammoths, saber-toothed cats, short-faced bears, ground sloths, and many other animals roamed free. Roughly 10,000 to 20,000 years ago, Los Angeles was thought to have had a cooler, damper climate, where pits of asphalt or tar bubbled up to the surface. Animals would find themselves trapped in the sticky substance, attracting predators to a feast. Some predators in turn would also become trapped. As thousands of years passed, these animals' bones became preserved in the thick tar pools, leaving a scientific goldmine just waiting to be discovered.

La Brea Tar Pits is the only active Ice Age excavation site in the world set in an urban location. At the turn of the twentieth century, geologist

The La Brea Tar Pits & Museum is at 5801 Wilshire Boulevard.

W.W. Orcutt and scientist F.M. Anderson uncovered fossilized bones in the area and realized they had discovered much more than just a tar pit. Their find sparked over a decade of excavations where over 750,000 specimens of plants and animals were found in roughly 100 sites. This led to over a century of scientific discoveries at the site, one of the more recent discoveries being in 2006 when more fossils were uncovered during the construction of a parking lot. The geological phenomenon and historic treasure trove of La Brea Tar Pits is truly a sight to behold and helps one understand what the Los Angeles area was like thousands and thousands of years ago.

MID CITY

It's hard to imagine, but oil derricks once littered the entire Mid City region (as well as other parts of Los Angeles). In the 1890s, Arthur Gilmore, a dairy farmer, found oil on his land near La Brea Tar Pits. The field was named the Salt Lake Oil Field, and by 1917 there were more than 450 wells in the area, which produced millions of barrels of oil. Other oil fields in the area were Los 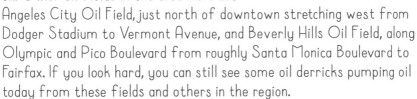 Angeles City Oil Field, just north of downtown stretching west from Dodger Stadium to Vermont Avenue, and Beverly Hills Oil Field, along Olympic and Pico Boulevard from roughly Santa Monica Boulevard to Fairfax. If you look hard, you can still see some oil derricks pumping oil today from these fields and others in the region.

As oil fields popped up all over Mid City at the turn of the century, so too did residential neighborhoods. The early 1900s saw a boom for development away from the downtown core, largely due to the trolley systems that could easily bring people to work downtown and home again in these less developed areas. Some of the residential neighborhoods here, such as Larchmont Village, LaFayette Square, Victoria Park, and Hancock Park, are fantastic areas to explore. These neighborhoods boast tree-lined streets and beautiful homes.

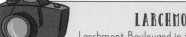

LARCHMONT BOULEVARD

Larchmont Boulevard in the heart of Larchmont Village has a cute main street lined with restaurants, cafés, bookstores, and boutiques. Take a break touring, grab a coffee, and snap a few photos. Later you will marvel that despite looking like you were in a small town, you were actually in the heart of Los Angeles!

THE MIRACLE MILE

In 1921, developer A. W. Ross saw through the rural, unpaved portion of Wilshire Boulevard (between Fairfax and La Brea) filled with oil derricks and bean farms, and envisioned a commercial district filled with retail opportunities. He noticed personal automobiles were on the rise and watched as neighboring Beverly Hills and Hollywood exploded with development. Ross began developing the area with a few small store fronts and a two-story building. By 1928, the strip was named the "Miracle Mile," which some at the time ironically thought was appropriate as it would take a miracle for Ross's vision to be successful.

Within a year of earning the moniker, major department stores began to migrate from the core and build gorgeous Art Deco buildings along Wilshire to showcase their goods. The move from downtown allowed for ample parking and more space, a dream for shoppers. The first store to arrive was Desmond's, and then Bullocks Wilshire in 1929. Coulter's (at Hauser & Wilshire, though the original building no longer exists) and The May Company soon followed.

But starting in the 1960s, shopping experiences moved to the malls, and the once popular department stores turned into apartments or offices. The area was no longer a retail destination but had become rundown. Luckily, revival in the 1980s came again to the Miracle Mile when museums found their way

Bullocks Wilshire is at 3050 Wilshire Boulevard.

to Wilshire and created Museum Row. Replacing some of the old department stores (the May Company is now the Academy Museum of Motion Pictures) and revamping or building new interesting structures (Petersen Automotive Museum), Ross's vision for this stretch along Wilshire once again is a top destination for tourists and Angelenos to visit.

A MID-CENTURY MARVEL

One of the best examples of Googie architecture along the Miracle Mile, Johnie's Coffee Shop has been most obviously a coffee shop to more recently a volunteer office for Bernie Sanders's presidential campaign runs (in 2016 and 2020). It has also been used in several movies and music videos such as *The Big Lebowski* and Tom Petty and the Heartbreaker's "Swingin'" music video.

Johnie's Coffee Shop is at 6101 Wilshire Boulevard.

MUSEUM ROW
& NEARBY ATTRACTIONS

Immerse yourself in all the art, science, and culture offered just a few miles of each other!

- Academy Museum of Motion Pictures
- Craft Contemporary
- La Brea Tar Pits & George C. Page Museum
- Los Angeles County Museum of Art (LACMA)
- Petersen Automotive Museum
- Zimmer Children's Museum

The Petersen Automotive Museum is at 6060 Wilshire Boulevard.

ENTER: Film Director

A film director manages all creative aspects of a film to ensure their vision of the screenplay is captured. In pre-production, the film director meets with casting, set, props, costume, and makeup departments to relay their ideas. While in production, they work with cinematography, camera, stage, and lighting crews, as well as directly with the actors to ensure their visualization is upheld. During post-production, they collaborate with film editors, special effects, and sound and music departments. The film director is responsible for the film's biggest creative decisions, which ultimately may lead to the success or failure of a production.

Now imagine you have just won the Academy Award for Best Director. You've had several movie flops and some successes, yet finally feel as a director, this film represents your finest work. Fill in the prompts to help craft your acceptance speech.

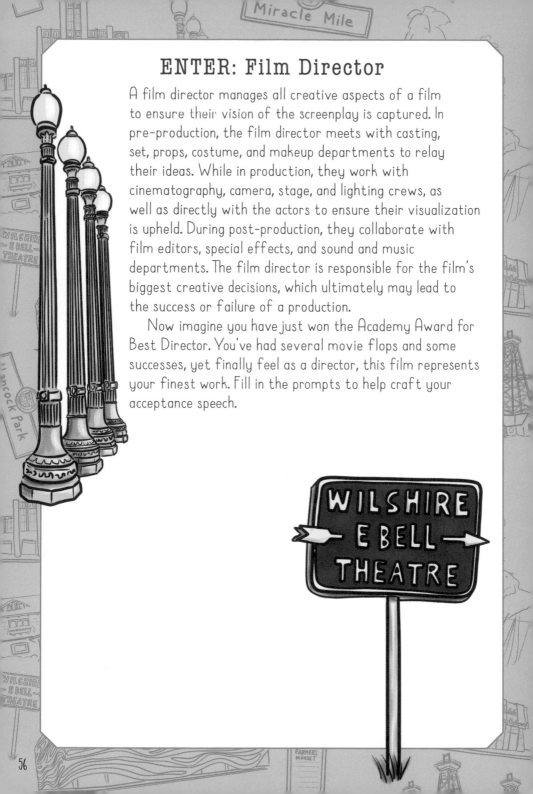

YOUR ACCEPTANCE SPEECH
FOR BEST DIRECTOR

Best Director

_____! _____! _____!
[Exclamation]   [Exclamation]   [Exclamation]

What an _____ honor to be given this award. After
                [adjective]

years of making _____ films, I finally found the
                    [film genre]

_____ screenplay, _____. This story was
[adjective]   [movie title]

meant to be told to _____. With the outstanding guidance
                        [location]

of my fellow directors, _____ and _____, I was able
                            [name]   [name]

to bring the tale of a down-and-out _____ to life and help
                                        [profession]

them blossom into a _____.
                        [profession]

First, I'd like to thank _____, _____, and
                            [family member's name]   [pet's name]

_____, I wouldn't be here without your _____
[best friend's name]   [adjective]

love and support. Second, I'd like to thank _____,
                                                [teacher's name]

my _____ teacher in _____ grade. Without their
    [school subject]   [grade level]

guidance I would not have learned the art of _____.
                                                [school subject]

To the entire cast and crew, _____,
                                [famous person]

_____, _____, your talent is
[famous person]   [famous person]

_____, and I am honored to work with you.
[adjective]

Thank you to the _____ for this nomination and
                    [organization]

award. I will proudly put this statue in my _____,
                                                [room in your house]

next to my other _____. And before the exit
                    [objects in your house]

music, _____, plays, I just want to get in one last word.
        [song title]

We must keep fighting for _____ and
                            [political movement]

_____. Our planet, _____,
[world issue]   [planet name]

depends on it. _____!!
                [campaign slogan]

ECHO PARK, SILVER LAKE & LOS FELIZ

Tucked between Downtown Los Angeles and Hollywood and nestled among the hills are three sought-after enclaves: Echo Park, Silver Lake, and Los Feliz (including Griffith Park). These artsy and diverse neighborhoods are filled with an eclectic mix of cultures and are home to some of the best recreation areas and views in all of LA.

FROM RANCH LAND TO PARK

These neighborhoods were part of one of the first land grants in California dating back to the Spanish colonial days in 1795. The Spanish governor granted the 6,500-plus acres to José Vicente Feliz, naming the concession Rancho Los Feliz. Then in the late 1800s, Colonel Griffith Jenkins Griffith acquired over 4,000 acres of the Rancho and donated over 3,000 of them to the City of Los Angeles for use as a public park. The land was renamed Griffith Park in his honor.

Despite Griffith's altruism, there was a darker side to his story. In 1903, he shot his wife and was sent to prison at San Quentin. Once he was out, he returned to Los Angeles and again gave money to the city to create a Greek theatre

Griffith Observatory is at 2800 E Observatory Road.

and a hall of science. The offer was rejected this time, but Griffith left the same gift in his will to the City, which eventually accepted it in 1919 after Griffith's death.

MOVIE STUDIOS MOVE IN

When the rancho era ended, the film industry took hold in Los Feliz, Silver Lake, and Echo Park (once known as Edendale) just as it was happening in adjacent Hollywood. Walt Disney built his first studio in Silver Lake (now a Gelson's Market), and Disney supposedly drew his first images of Mickey Mouse in his uncle's garage in Los Feliz. Mack Sennett set up Keystone Studios in Echo Park and many silent stars worked in the area, including Charlie Chaplin, Gloria Swanson, and Fatty Arbuckle. Even Laurel and Hardy danced along the staircases in Silver Lake in their movie *The Music Box*.

The Music Box steps are between Descanso Drive & Vendome Street, across Laurel and Hardy Park.

As the decades moved on, so too did many of the studios looking for larger plots of land. Now only a few still remain, namely The Prospect Studios. Starting in the 1930s, many LGBTQ members found supportive communities in Silver Lake and Echo Park where they could express their individuality in a time when it was not accepted. In fact, Silver Lake is where one of the first gay organizations in the country, The Mattachine Society, was founded in 1950. Latino families also found a supportive community in Echo Park and Silver Lake and benefited from the proximity to downtown.

Although gentrification has displaced many, much of the neighborhoods still retain their bohemian charm. Be sure to take the afternoon and wander these historic streets, from their main commercial strips to the hidden gems within, to capture the fabulous views and sites.

NEIGHBORHOOD DETAILS

ECHO PARK Historic Echo Park is more than just home to Dodger Stadium! There's loads of artsy charm along Sunset Boulevard between Echo Park Avenue and Mohawk Street, plus nature and views at beautiful Echo Park Lake.

SILVER LAKE Silver Lake is most often known for the Silver Lake Reservoir. Although you are not able to get on the water, there is a great trail to walk around it and soak up the surrounding neighborhood. Also visit Sunset Boulevard, Glendale Boulevard, and Hyperion Avenue for endless restaurant, bar, and café options as well as artsy boutiques and gift stores.

LOS FELIZ In Los Feliz you will find famous homes such as Frank Lloyd Wright's Ennis Home and the Lovell House, as well as Walt Disney's home on Woking Way. Vermont and Hillhurst Avenue make up the commercial section. Shops, bars, restaurants, and a few historic charmers like the historic Los Feliz Theatre line these fun streets to stroll.

SNOW WHITE COTTAGES

It's unclear whether these tiny cottages on Griffith Park, close to Walt Disney's early studios, inspired Disney's *Snow White and the Seven Dwarfs*... but they sure look the part! The Snow White Cottages are at 2906 Griffith Park Boulevard.

GRIFFITH PARK

What makes Griffith Park so unique is its hilly, mountainous terrain. For the most part, the park amenities are nestled on peaks and in valleys that offer incredible views of the city and an urban outdoor adventure unlike any other place.

Probably the most recognizable feature is the Griffith Observatory. This stunning Greek Revival–Art Deco observatory offers

WELCOME TO GRIFFITH PARK

free admission to exhibit halls and charges only a small fee for planetarium shows. The surrounding grounds have gorgeous views to the ocean (on clear days) and also offer a close-up look at the famed Hollywood sign.

The Greek Theatre's first show in 1931 was an operatic performance attended by almost 4,000 patrons. Today, the Greek Theatre books big names in the music and entertainment industry.

But there are several more sites to explore within Griffith Park.

- **LOS ANGELES ZOO & BOTANICAL GARDENS**: The Griffith Park Zoo first opened in 1912. Today's LA Zoo opened only a few miles from that original site and is a popular destination for kids of all ages.

- **GRIFFITH PARK PONY RIDES & PETTING ZOO**: Little ones will love a pony ride at this old-fashioned spot.
- **LOS ANGELES EQUESTRIAN CENTER**: Infamously used in the polo scene in the film *Pretty Woman*, the Los Angeles Equestrian Center offers many horse shows and events throughout the year.
- **BIRD SANCTUARY GRIFFITH PARK**: Find hiking trails and picnic for the perfect spot to birdwatch and relax in the park.
- **GOLF, TENNIS, & HIKING**: The park offers two golf courses, various tennis courts, and numerous hikes for the active visitor.
- **AUTRY MUSEUM OF THE AMERICAN WEST**: This museum is dedicated to exploring the peoples and cultures of the American West.
- **GRIFFITH PARK MERRY-GO-ROUND**: Built in 1926, this ornate merry-go-round features 68 decorated horses and an impressive organ that plays over 1,500 marches and waltzes.
- **TRAIN ATTRACTIONS**: The Los Angeles Live Streamers Railroad Museum was founded in 1956 by a group of train enthusiasts who wanted to share their enthusiasm for train history to the public. The Griffith Park Train Rides have been delighting young ones since 1948! The Travel Town Museum celebrates the history of railroads in the Los Angeles region as well as the Southwest of the United States.

ENTER: Property Master, or Props Master

Head of the property department or a senior member of the art department, the props master on a film set is responsible for buying and acquiring, creating, managing, and ultimately placing and overseeing usage of all props needed for a production. They must research details to ensure the items are appropriate and realistic to the era and location of the film, from labels on food products to accuracy of automobiles or computers in a scene. They must also ensure the prop performs as expected and holds up after successive usages throughout the filming.

You are the props master for a film about three creative friends who live together in the Los Feliz/Silver Lake/Echo Park area. One of the characters works as a hairstylist, one works at their family's Mexican restaurant, and one is an entry-level set designer in the entertainment industry. They all are fiercely independent, desperately trying to make their mark on the world, yet struggling to make ends meet. Wander in and out of the vintage stores, boutiques, bars, cafés, and restaurants of these neighborhoods to find the perfect props for this film. Draw each prop you find and describe its purpose in the film.

Prop Name:
Purpose:

Prop Name:
Purpose:

Prop Name:
Purpose:

Prop Name:
Purpose:

Prop Name:
Purpose:

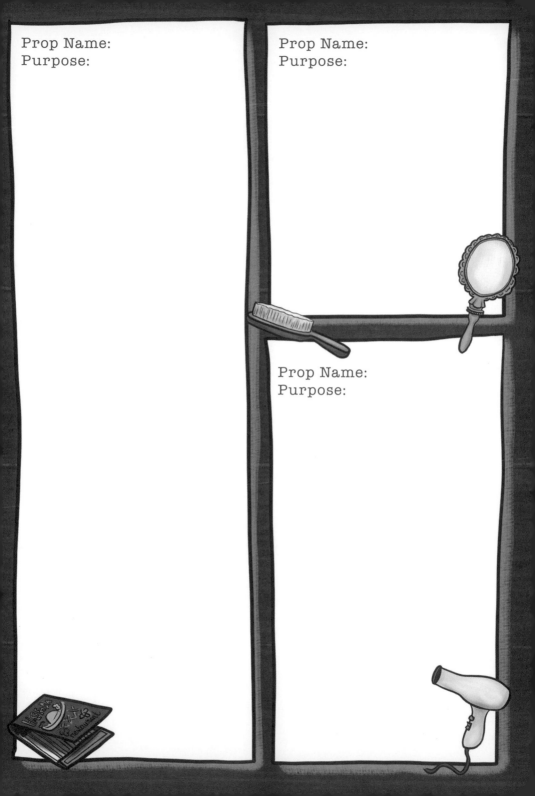

CHINATOWN, LITTLE TOKYO & KOREATOWN

Driving around Los Angeles is like being able to travel to different parts of the world. It's amazing you can have all these experiences within the city limits of Los Angeles—and all without a passport!

CHINATOWN

The first two Chinese people to appear on the Los Angeles census was in 1850. By 1870, there were 200 Chinese people, and 30 years later there were 3,000 Chinese living in Los Angeles. They worked as laborers building the railroads and were instrumental in farming produce and providing everyday services such as laundry and restaurants to inhabitants. They lived in the area that is now called Old Chinatown, adjacent to the pueblo and where present-day Union Station is.

Then in 1882 Congress passed the Chinese Exclusion Act, which stopped immigration from China for decades and spurred city residents to boycott Chinese goods and services. By the 1930s, the city decided to tear down dilapidated Old Chinatown in favor of a centralized railroad station. Determined to maintain their community, some prominent Chinese Americans joined forces and secured nearby land to move to, naming the neighborhood New Chinatown (today's Chinatown).

New Chinatown opened in 1938 as the first neighborhood to be planned and owned solely by Chinese Americans. Driving down Broadway today, you can see the hustle and bustle of daily life, with busy stores, markets, restaurants, and businesses. The heart of the neighborhood is Central Plaza, which is filled with shops, restaurants, and galleries. Although many Chinese American

families have moved out to the suburbs, Chinatown remains a bustling center for commerce and a rich reminder of the perseverance and prosperity this community brings to the region.

LITTLE TOKYO

Little Tokyo, located near the Civic Center in DTLA, is a small, tightknit community that has prospered and persevered for over a century despite extreme discrimination and hardships. The early Japanese immigrants to Los Angeles brought many new skills to the area in farming (specifically produce), fishing, and flowers. They set up thriving businesses and celebrated their heritage while also embracing life in America.

During World War II, Executive Order 9066 imprisoned Japanese Americans in camps and destroyed their way of life in Little Tokyo. LA's Japanese communities emptied out overnight, businesses shut, and goods were eliminated. Many African Americans who migrated west to work in the wartime defense industry moved into these empty neighborhoods. Little Tokyo soon became known as "Bronzeville."

After the war, determined Japanese Americans returned to Little Tokyo and revitalized their community. Today, Little Tokyo is a thriving neighborhood. At the heart of the neighborhood is a two-block area interlaced with pedestrian streets filled with a wide variety of Japanese restaurants, shops, and a two-story mall, Japanese Village Plaza.

Across the street is the Japanese American National Museum. If you happen to be in Los Angeles in August, be sure to experience the popular Nisei Week in which the town celebrates their culture and community with parades and a variety of events.

MORE TO EXPLORE

These neighborhoods are well worth the visit when you're in the area.

- Little Bangladesh (Near Koreatown)
- Historic Filipinotown—HiFi (Near Echo Park)
- Little Armenia & Thai Town (Near Hollywood)
- Little Ethiopia (Near Mid-City)

KOREATOWN

With roughly 125,000 residents, Koreatown (aka K-Town) is one of the densest communities in LA County and one of the most diverse. Just a little over 30% of its population is of Korean descent while Latinos make up over 50%.

Korean immigration to America came in three waves. The first wave followed after diplomatic relations were formed between the US and Korea in 1882. The number of Koreans in America remained very low during the first decades of the century as the Asian Exclusion Act of 1924 prevented more immigrants from arriving. The few Koreans in Los Angeles were initially centered around Bunker Hill near downtown, but by the 1930s they settled near what became known as Old Koreatown.

The second, larger wave came during the mid-century following the Korean War, with most Korean immigrants in LA residing in Old Koreatown. The third wave happened between the 1960s to 1980s, with more than half of the Koreans in America choosing to make Los Angeles their home. Freeway construction and neighborhood changes in Old Koreatown spurred residents to find a new neighborhood to build their community in the Mid-Wilshire area. Having faced different levels of discrimination since their arrival a hundred years earlier, Koreatown suffered one of its biggest tragedies during the 1992 Los Angeles riots in response to the beating and arrest of Rodney King. With over 2,000 Korean businesses destroyed, many residents fled to the suburbs, but many stayed and faced a tough several years rebuilding their community.

Today, Koreatown in Los Angeles remains a core beacon of community across the United States. Being the first Koreatown outside of Korea, it carries a legacy and history of what hard work and determination means, and is a prime location for trendy food spots and bars around the area.

The Koreatown Galleria is at 3250 W Olympic Boulevard.

CULTURAL MUSEUMS

There are several museums dedicated to the cultures that make Los Angeles.
- California African American Museum
- Chinese American Museum
- Italian American Museum of Los Angeles
- Japanese American Museum
- Korean Cultural Center
- Korean American National Museum
- LA Plaza de Cultura y Artes
- Martial Arts History Museum
- Museum of African American Art
- Museum of Latin American Art
- Pacific Island Ethnic Art Museum
- Skirball Cultural Center
- Southwest Museum of the American Indian
- USC Pacific Asia Museum

ENTER: Location Scout

A location scout brings a screenplay to life by researching and finding the best environments to shoot scenes or an entire film. They have to contact property owners, check permission requirements, and ensure proper lighting, sound, and availability of electricity, as well as scout out parking for the crew and the equipment. Once the locations have been approved, the location scout manages all legal issues and permits, and shares any location details to set and prop crews to ensure the location is ready for filming. After filming, they make sure the location is returned to its normal state.

You are the location scout for *The Dynasty Heist*, a new fast-paced action film about Asian antiquity thefts. You unfortunately don't have the funds to head overseas to film, so you must find the perfect local spots to film key scenes in the movie. Fill out the worksheet here providing details about the location (street names, buildings, businesses, etc.) and why it is perfect for the scenes. Create a quick sketch or snap a photo to remember the location.

SCENE	LOCATION	SKETCH & NOTES
The main star, Amaya, recruits their band of high-tech thieves and art heist experts from an unsuspecting teahouse or café.		
Amaya and their partner Dae stake out one of the many Chinatown galleries to hide their stolen multimillion-dollar goods in plain sight.		
FBI agent Chris spots Amaya and Dae at a shopping mall, and a chase ensues.		
Chris and Amaya tensely yet respectfully come to terms after the case is dismissed while sharing a delicious meal at a family-run restaurant.		

PASADENA

Tucked up against the San Gabriel Mountains and neighbor to Los Angeles, Pasadena started as a resort town luring Midwesterners to winter in a warmer climate, but developed into a distinct community that had all the amenities needed to stand out on its own.

The San Gabriel Mission is at 428 S Mission Drive.

HAHAMONGNA AND THE SPANIARDS

Pasadena was home to the Hahamongna tribe who lived in villages along the Arroyo Seco and in the canyons of the hills surrounding the San Gabriel Valley. When the Spaniards arrived, they built the San Gabriel Mission in 1771, the fourth mission out of 21 built up and down the California coast to strengthen the Spaniards' territory as well as convert the Native people to Catholicism.

ROSES, PARADES & SPORTS

Pasadena may not have its own national football or major league baseball team, but it is still home to the "Granddaddy" of postseason college football.

TOURNAMENT OF ROSES PARADE In 1890, the Valley Hunt Club of Pasadena looked to promote their midwinter tournament of games (including chariot races, jousting, polo, etc.) to Midwesterners and Easterners. They came up with the idea of a parade to kick off the games and show how bountiful, warm, and charming Pasadena winters were. They decorated show-stopping carriages with hundreds of colorful blooms, and over the next few years added motorized floats and marching bands.

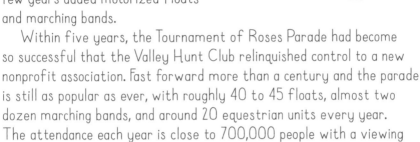

Within five years, the Tournament of Roses Parade had become so successful that the Valley Hunt Club relinquished control to a new nonprofit association. Fast forward more than a century and the parade is still as popular as ever, with roughly 40 to 45 floats, almost two dozen marching bands, and around 20 equestrian units every year. The attendance each year is close to 700,000 people with a viewing audience of approximately 70 million more.

THE ROSE BOWL & THE ROSE BOWL GAME

The first postseason football game, was held January 1, 1902 as a way to help fund the popular Rose Parade. Because Midwest team Michigan easily won against Stanford in a 49-0 game, football didn't return to the tournament games again until 14 years later, when it became an annual tradition. The game quickly grew popular, and on January 1, 1923, the newly built Rose Bowl stadium hosted the first Rose Bowl Game (USC vs. Penn State). The Rose Bowl has been reconfigured many times over the years but remained the largest football stadium in the United States until 1998. The stadium also hosted many other sporting events such as Olympic events, Super Bowls, and FIFA World Cup soccer finals, though it is still most known for the annual postseason Rose Bowl Game.

ROSE BOWL FLEA MARKET
Held once a month, this open air market draws nearly 20,000 people browsing roughly 2,500 vendors' goods. It has been an institution in Pasadena since it started.

BRAINIACS & SPACE NERDS

Pasadena has both brawn and brain, making it a unique place for people of all interests to visit.

CALIFORNIA INSTITUTE OF TECHNOLOGY

California Institute of Technology, or Caltech, is one of the strongest science and engineering schools in the nation. Its alumni, faculty, and

Caltech is at 1200 E California Boulevard.

researchers have received highly esteemed awards including the Nobel Laureate, Fields Medal, Turing Award, and National Medal of Science of Technology. Even Albert Einstein taught here as a visiting professor from 1931 to 1933.

JET PROPULSION LAB

Managed for NASA by Caltech, Jet Propulsion Lab (JPL) is a research facility that develops and conducts robotic space and Earth science missions.

JPL is at 4800 Oak Grove Drive.

Started by a group of students experimenting with rockets in the mid-1930s, JPL launched America's first satellite, created interplanetary spacecraft, and has sent robotic missions to study the moon, planets, comets, and asteroids.

HALE SOLAR LABORATORY

This astronomical observatory built in 1923 was originally the laboratory of George Ellery Hale, one of the pioneers who developed the discipline of astrophysics. The building is now a National Historic Landmark.

FOOD & A FORK IN THE ROAD

Pasadena boasts over 500 eateries—good to know you won't go hungry when exploring this city! But why is Pasadena such a food town? One can only speculate...

JULIA CHILD Pasadena is the birthplace of one of the best chefs, cooking teachers, and authors in the world, Julia Child. One of her first homes was at 625 Magnolia Avenue and it is said she spent most of her formative childhood years in Pasadena.

HOME OF THE CHEESEBURGER The cheeseburger was presumably first created in Pasadena in 1926. Working at his father's restaurant, once located at Fair Oaks and Colorado Boulevard, Lionel Sternberger added cheese to a burger, and the rest is history. The town is so proud of this fact that every January they host Cheeseburger Week!

A FORK IN THE ROAD Located at a literal fork in the road (South Pasadena Avenue and South St. John Avenue at Bellefontaine) is an 18-foot fork sculpture. First placed there without city permission, it was promptly removed, yet by popular demand it was put back.

BUNGALOW HEAVEN, MANSIONS & A CASTLE

One thing you can't miss when touring this city is the influence of the Arts and Crafts Movement. As Victorian architecture faded, Craftsman-style homes flourished. Pasadena is home to close to a thousand such homes, many of which are in a Historic Landmark District known as Bungalow Heaven (surrounding McDonald Park).

THE GAMBLE HOUSE: This stately Arts and Crafts-style home was built for Procter & Gamble heir David Gamble and his wife in 1908. It is now a museum and has been featured in many films, including *Back to the Future*.

The Gamble House is at 4 Westmoreland Pl.

WRIGLEY MANSION: Once home to chewing gum king William Wrigley Jr., this Renaissance three-story mansion is now the headquarters of the Pasadena Tournament of the Roses Association. The grounds are open to the public, and the house can be toured on specific days.

FENYES MANSION: This Beaux Arts home, built in 1906, has been featured in many films and is available for public tours.

ENTER: Screenwriter

A screenwriter creates a storyline, defines characters, and writes dialog that becomes the screenplay used to make a film. Sometimes the story is original work, and other times the screenwriter might adapt a story from an existing work, like a book, a play, or another film. The screenplay contains not only the dialog between characters but also details regarding the characters' moods as well as the physical setting.

You've been charged to write a scene for *May the Best Float Win*, a new mashup comedy film set in Pasadena. The film is about three friends: a mathematician from Caltech, a rocket scientist from JPL, and a young architect. They have been asked to design a float in the upcoming Rose Parade, and the antics ensue. Write a script of a scene where the mathematician, the scientist, and the architect argue over the theme of their float and what types of flowers they should use.

TIPS FOR WRITING THIS SCENE

Below are a few tips to keep in mind when writing the scene of your screenplay.

KNOW YOUR AUDIENCE. Before beginning your scene, decide who your audience is for your screenplay. Perhaps your scene is for hip twenty-year-olds, or perhaps you are writing for nostalgic sixty-year-olds. By understanding your audience, you can engage them in the dialog and action from the very beginning.

KNOW YOUR CHARACTERS. Think about how your characters talk and walk, what they eat, what they do for fun, their point of view, their quirks, etc. How is their personality portrayed in their dialog?

KNOW YOUR SETTING. With the Tournament of Roses in mind, add tidbits about the setting in your dialog and scene to create believability in your work.

LET YOUR CHARACTERS DRIVE THE STORY. Like every good writer knows, "show, don't tell" your audience what is happening. Your characters should guide the storyline, not the events. Let them react to situations and make their own choices.

May the Best Float Win Screenplay

[location]:

[scene/action]:

AMUSEMENT PARKS

With year-round temperate weather and the entertainment industry at its feet, it's no wonder Los Angeles is home to some of the best amusement parks in the world! In 1887, just south of DTLA, Washington Gardens opened hosting weekly variety shows and animal displays. By 1899, it had become Chutes Park with a baseball diamond and soon added hot air balloon rides, a roller coaster, a monkey circus, and a giant boat waterslide. In Pasadena, Busch Gardens opened in 1906 next to the Busch family mansion.

Along the waterfront, pleasure piers like the Million Dollar Pier, Ocean Park Pier, and Santa Monica Pier attracted crowds, while Venice of America drew thousands of visitors on the weekends. There were also loads of attractions featuring animals, such as Jungleland, Gay's Lion Farm, Ponyland, and the Los Angeles Alligator Farm. Over time, some of these piers and parks went under or closed, while others were refurbished and reopened with different names.

By the 1940s and '50s, amusement parks in Los Angeles had clearly come of age. Walter and Cordelia Knott's roadside berry and pie stand ballooned into Knott's Berry Farm, a year-round "county fair" and ghost town. Walt Disney's concept for a tourist attraction became a reality when Disneyland opened in July 1955. Universal Studios Hollywood expanded its various backstage studio tour operations in 1961 by offering "Glamor Trams" that included stops to see costumes, makeup presentations, star dressing rooms, and stunt shows.

Latecomer Legoland California entered the amusement park scene in 1999 as the first Legoland park outside of Europe.

Today, amusement parks can even include immersive cinematic experiences and sophisticated technology-driven rides. For example, at Disneyland's *Star Wars: Galaxy's Edge* the park guest becomes an actor in roaming the remote outpost on the planet Batuu. At Universal Studios Hollywood's *The Wizarding World of Harry Potter*, park employees dress as characters, and the park setting and rides combine to offer real experiences for park guests to participate in the magical world.

As for roller coasters and thrill rides, these are still as popular as ever. Six Flags Magic Mountain even holds the record for the most roller coasters in an amusement park. So, head out to one of the many amusement parks in the Los Angeles area and lose yourself in an adventure!

ENTER: Concept Designer or Theme Park Engineer

A concept designer for location-based entertainment (LBE) or theme park engineer creates theme park rides and experiences. LBE can range broadly from rides at an amusement park to museum installations or live entertainment. Concept designers

DAY PASS

amusement park

design real-world experiences and typically have art, theatre, or set design backgrounds. With the same creative energy, theme park engineers design with their extensive structural, electrical, and mechanical engineering knowledge as well as programming, physics, and mathematical skills.

You've been tasked to design the next great amusement park. What's the theme of your park? What stories do you want your guests to experience? What rides will you design? Create a map of your new amusement park.

THE JOURNAL

BEST OF LOS ANGELES

Fill out the lists below with your favorites from exploring Los Angeles.

BEST SIGHTS

_____
_____
_____
_____
_____
_____
_____
_____
_____

BEST EATS

_____
_____
_____
_____
_____
_____
_____
_____
_____

BEST SHOPPING

_____
_____
_____
_____
_____
_____
_____
_____
_____

BEST DRINKS & NIGHTLIFE

_____
_____
_____
_____
_____
_____
_____
_____
_____

BEST PARKS

_____
_____
_____
_____
_____
_____
_____
_____
_____
_____

BEST MUSEUMS

_____
_____
_____
_____
_____
_____
_____
_____
_____
_____

The Malibu Pier is off the Pacific Coast Highway, 11 miles west of Santa Monica.

 **DAY**
#____

DATE _____

RATING ☆☆☆☆☆

WEATHER   ☂

PLACES VISITED

_____
_____
_____
_____
_____
_____
_____
_____
_____

BEST EATS OF THE DAY

_____
_____
_____
_____
_____

QUOTE OF THE DAY

_____
_____
_____
_____

ONLY IN LA

_____
_____
_____

SOMETHING I SAW TODAY

 # DAY
#_____

DATE _____   RATING ☆☆☆☆☆

WEATHER

 PLACES VISITED

_____
_____
_____
_____
_____
_____
_____
_____
_____

BEST EATS OF THE DAY

_____
_____
_____
_____
_____
_____
_____
_____

" " QUOTE OF THE DAY

_____
_____
_____
_____

ONLY IN LA

_____
_____
_____
_____

SOMETHING I SAW TODAY

 **DAY**

_____

DATE _____ **RATING** ☆☆☆☆☆

WEATHER

PLACES VISITED

_____
_____
_____
_____
_____
_____
_____
_____
_____

BEST EATS OF THE DAY

_____
_____
_____
_____

QUOTE OF THE DAY

_____
_____
_____

ONLY IN LA

_____
_____
_____

SOMETHING I SAW TODAY

DAY
#____

DATE _____ RATING ☆☆☆☆☆

WEATHER

PLACES VISITED

_____
_____
_____
_____
_____
_____
_____
_____
_____

BEST EATS OF THE DAY

_____
_____
_____
_____
_____
_____
_____

QUOTE OF THE DAY

_____
_____
_____
_____

ONLY IN LA

_____
_____
_____
_____

SOMETHING I SAW TODAY

DAY

#____

DATE _____ RATING ☆☆☆☆☆

WEATHER

 PLACES VISITED

_____
_____
_____
_____
_____
_____
_____
_____
_____

BEST EATS OF THE DAY

_____
_____
_____
_____
_____
_____
_____

QUOTE OF THE DAY

_____
_____
_____
_____

ONLY IN LA

_____
_____

SOMETHING I SAW TODAY

DAY

_____

DATE _____   RATING ☆☆☆☆☆

WEATHER

PLACES VISITED

_____
_____
_____
_____
_____
_____
_____
_____
_____

BEST EATS OF THE DAY

_____
_____
_____
_____
_____
_____

QUOTE OF THE DAY

_____
_____
_____
_____

ONLY IN LA

_____
_____
_____
_____

SOMETHING I SAW TODAY

DAY

#_____

DATE _____

RATING ☆☆☆☆☆

WEATHER

PLACES VISITED

_____
_____
_____
_____
_____
_____
_____
_____
_____

BEST EATS OF THE DAY

_____
_____
_____
_____
_____
_____

QUOTE OF THE DAY

_____
_____
_____
_____

ONLY IN LA

_____
_____

SOMETHING I SAW TODAY

PALM TREES EVERYWHERE
With the exception of the California Fan palm, palm trees are actually not native to Los Angeles. They were initially brought by the Franciscan missionaries as ornamental plants, but the palms proliferated and flourished across the LA basin, and were used to promote the "tropical" lifestyle look.

LA
FASHION SCENE

Not only is Los Angeles creatively fueled by the entertainment business while acting as a melting pot of cultures that influence style, it also houses some of the best clothing manufacturing in the country, from cut-and-sew companies to top-end washhouses that serve lines like the premium denim industry.

_____

_____

_____

_____

_____

_____

_____

_____

_____

_____

_____

_____

_____

_____

_____

_____

_____

_____

_____

_____

_____

_____

_____

_____

_____

_____

_____

_____

_____

_____

_____

_____

_____

_____

_____

_____

_____

_____

_____

_____

_____

_____

_____

CLASSIC LA SURF MOVIES

The Endless Summer
Gidget
Beach Blanket Bingo
Blazing Boards
Point Break
Riding Giants
View from a Blue Moon
Bethany Hamilton: Unstoppable
Surf's Up

VALLEY GIRL
In 1982, musician Frank Zappa released a song titled "Valley Girl" featuring his then 14-year-old daughter, Moon Unit, saying typical teen girl phrases heard in the San Fernando Valley during that time. Intended to poke fun at the superficial nature of the upper-middle-class girls of the Valley, the song ended up only reinforcing the ditzy banter and increasing popularity of the trend. It even inspired the 1983 cult classic movie *Valley Girl*.

PACIFIC DESIGN CENTER

In 1975, the huge Pacific Design
Center opened in West Hollywood
to support the design needs of
the nearby entertainment and
arts communities. The building
houses over a million square
feet of showrooms displaying
the latest in furnishings, fabrics,
wall covering, lighting, kitchen and bath products,
and floors, and even hosts a branch of the
Museum of Contemporary Art.

HOLLYWOOD BOWL

Even back in the 1910s and '20s early Hollywood residents recognized the unique musical, theatrical, and religious venue they had nestled in the Hollywood Hills. The Hollywood Bowl's iconic shell has gone through several transformations over the century, yet besides the very first pyramid-shaped stage which was quickly torn down, it has remained relatively the same. The Hollywood Bowl is at 2301 N Highland Avenue.

_____

_____

_____

_____

_____

_____

_____

_____

_____

_____

_____

_____

_____

_____

_____

_____

_____

_____

_____

_____

BILLBOARDS OF SUNSET STRIP
With the rise of the music scene in the 1960s and '70s, the Sunset Strip became the mecca for huge billboards touting the latest and greatest rock stars. Product advertising, film debuts, and other entertainment were also displayed, but musicians and their albums got the most attention.

Today, the billboards along this short stretch of Sunset Boulevard command top dollar in the billboard world (second only to billboards in New York's Times Square).

DEDICATION

To Natalie, my creative travel partner and artistic soul mate, I am so very lucky to have you as my daughter. From the countless number of letters you wrote to the fairies in our yard to your Rococo photo shoots, you bring so much imagination to this world. I love exploring every nook and cranny with you, searching for one-of-a-kind color palettes, cool aesthetics, and unique vibes. As you head off on your own, I can't wait to watch you share your talents with the rest of the world and look forward to the many artsy adventures in our future.

Also known as the 110 and the Pasadena Freeway, Arroyo Seco Parkway is the first freeway built in the United States and connects to Route 66. Drive through to visit Pasadena and more!

Text and Illustrations © 2021 by Betsy Beier

Published by West Margin Press®

WEST MARGIN PRESS

WestMarginPress.com

WEST MARGIN PRESS
Publishing Director: Jennifer Newens
Marketing Manager: Alice Wertheimer
Project Specialist: Micaela Clark
Editor: Olivia Ngai
Design & Production: Rachel Lopez Metzger

LCCN: 2021936489

ISBN: 9781513267296

Proudly distributed by
Ingram Publisher Services

Printed in China
1 2 3 4 5